SACRED TIMES, TIMELESS SEASONS

A book of poetry and stories
Seeking and finding
God in our lives

by Gary J. Boelhower, Ph.D.

HI-TIME Publishing Corp.

Artwork: Dolores Ehr-Goetz

Dolores Ehr-Goetz, mother of five and grandmother of two, has painted professionally for thirty years. She has also created liturgical artwork and banners for seven years. For eleven years, she has been teaching elementary art in Catholic schools and is currently teaching in the Unified Catholic Parish Schools, Beaver Dam, Wisconsin.

Mrs. Ehr-Goetz is a catechist in the Confirmation program of St. Michael Parish, Beaver Dam, and is a student at Marian College, Fond du Lac. She and her husband Anthony live in rural Beaver Dam with their faithful cat, Angel.

Library of Congress Card Catalog Number 86-082885

ISBN: 0-937997-05-6

CONTENTS

DEDICATION

To my friend, my lover, my wife,
Patricia Lee Wahoske Boelhower
and the three unimaginable gifts
with which God has blessed our union,
Rebecca, Joel and Matthew.

HOW TO USE THIS BOOK

Why did Jesus teach in parables? Why did He tell stories that contained common images of seeds and soil, sheep and shepherds, birds and flowers? Was it because His audience couldn't comprehend other forms of discourse? I don't think so. Through the use of familiar images and surprising stories, Jesus was able to touch the hearts of people. There is a certain power in a story that invites participation. Jesus' use of common images enabled persons to experience the radical new vision of the kingdom.

To touch the hearts of people, to facilitate an experience of the original freshness of Christ's message is a challenge that parents, teachers and liturgical ministers face today. This book of poems and stories is offered as a resource to all those concerned with reflecting upon and communicating the Christian message.

Teachers and discussion leaders might use a story or poem as a discussion starter in a religion class or in a small group gathering. Many of the selections in this book were written in response to questions and challenges I received as a teacher. To the question "How does God talk to us?" I responded with the story "The Voice of God." When faced with the challenge "Why should we go to Mass?" I told the story "Remember." Confronting the task of communicating the profound mystery of God made flesh, I penned the poems "Promise of Love," "Christmas Story" and others included here. In an attempt to share my understanding of faith as a way of seeing reality, I composed the story "With Eyes Wide Open." It is my hope that these poems and stories might enable other teachers to communicate the Christian message in a way that invites involvement and continued exploration.

Homilists and planners of liturgical celebrations, too, might find these poems or stories appropriate resource material for sermons or meditation material for prayer services and the Eucharistic Liturgy. I have used several of the poems as introductions to prayer to set the theme or as meditations after Communion.

Many of the selections published here were simply expressions of the powerful, surprising presence of God, as my

6

eyes were opened to see things anew. I hope that they might be useful as resources for personal reflection and prayer.

A Scripture reference that continues the theme of the particular selection is given for each poem and story. These might be helpful in your private prayer or in creating prayer experiences for others.

TIMELESS SEASONS

Without seasons
there would be
only dry days of sameness —
no looking forward,
no music in the time.

Without seasons
there would be
only dull boredom —
no times for changes,
no new feelings or rearrangings.
Can you imagine a year
without Christmas or Easter,
without summer or fall?
Without seasons, there would be
no music in the time.

But there is a season for every purpose:
a time for trees and tinsel,
a time for baskets of candy,
a time for turkey and dressing,
a time for swimming and picnics.

A time for birth,
a time for dying,
a time for tears,
a time for rejoicing.

Each time is our time —
a season of our heart
that puts music in the time.

Ecclesiastes 3:1-8

INTRODUCTION

There is an ancient story that tells of a young man who wanted to speak with God. He was burdened with concerns and questions and distractions in his daily life. His time was filled with many tasks and many people. He wanted to get away from this hectic world to encounter God, who would certainly help him to make sense of it all. It was his understanding that he could speak with God at the top of the magnificent mountain that overlooked the valley of human love and conflict. There, he thought, God spent His days and nights overseeing the frantic comings and goings of all the people. His journey to the top of the mountain was long and arduous. But all his effort to escape from the sounds of laughter and weeping, struggling and singing that was going on in the valley would be worth it when he could meet God in the majestic silence at the top of the mountain.

When, finally, the young man reached the summit of the mountain he found it deserted. God was not there. The young man felt the depths of despair. Since there was no one to give meaning to his life, he decided to throw himself off the mountain. As the young man was poised ready to jump from the summit, he glanced down at the valley filled with old men and women, young girls and boys, babies being carried in the arms of their mothers and fathers, and, to his amazement, he spotted God in the midst of all the people. As he surveyed the hectic scene in the valley below, he saw the face of God lifted in full-throated laughter as a mother wiped a delicious mess of chocolate ice cream off the face of her little boy. He saw the hands of God reaching out in comfort as an elderly man stroked the gray hair of his dying wife. He saw the strong shoulders of God heave with effort as a builder fastened the cable of a new bridge. He noticed the wise eyes of God as a young woman poured over books in a library.

The young man realized that God lived in the valley of love and conflict, laughter and tears, struggle and peace. As he journeyed down the mountain, he promised himself that he would use his new vision to find meaning in the midst of God's people.

The underlying theme of this collection of poems and stories is the central truth of the Christian faith — incarnation. The profound mystery brought to light in the person of Jesus is that God is at home in our world. The experience of God that provides the foundation for this book is the experience of

Emmanuel — God with us.

Throughout much of Christian history, we have not allowed the life and message of Jesus to really shape our understanding of God. God has been largely understood as the unchangeable absolute in perfect control over the world. Most of our images of God have been of some gray-bearded, solemn patriarch ruling in majestic splendor. We have thought of God as a great judge who scrutinizes our actions and keeps track of our shortcomings. We have pictured Him as a stern lawgiver who exists on high.

Where in these images is the God revealed in Jesus — the God who becomes flesh, the powerless God who is hung on a cross? Where in these pictures is the Good Shepherd-God, the God who feels our every pain and joy? If we take the revelation of God in Jesus seriously, we are led to continually reshape our image of God.

We must rely on human words and human experiences to find the proper way to form an image of God. When we look at the best that we can be as humans, we have an indication of how we can most fruitfully think about God. The most authentic human experience is, of course, the experience of love. To love means to feel with another and to allow another's life to enter into our own. Love entails both acceptance and challenge as we share history and promise. The God I believe in is the God who fully feels our every nuance of pain and joy. The Christian God, it seems to me, never stops laughing and crying, suffering and hoping with all of us who are brothers and sisters of one family. In the past, the idea of God's perfection often meant God's removal from the world. However, the idea of God's perfection can also be articulated in terms of a perfectly loving being who enters into our world, into our lives and allows us to affect Him/Her. (It is important to recognize that the being of God must fully incorporate the richness of what we stereotypically term masculine and feminine characteristics.) Unlike humans who take into account only a small number of the vast experiences of the world, God fully and completely feels the totality of experience. God passionately appropriates every act, prayer, hope and dream in the universe.

God's being does not end in this depth of feeling, however. God's life is also that of saving gift. God challenges the world with possibility — with creative newness that can bring vitality and fresh life. For every experience that is shared, God offers the challenge of growth that draws us into deeper love and broader justice. God offers to us in each new moment of existence that perfect possibility, exactly relevant to our past experience, that beckons us into creative transformation.

This image of God as fully feeling and perfectly challenging implies a spirituality of the Christian life that is adventure. The Christian who models his or her life on this God-image sees the spiritual life as an ongoing personal process of responding to the possibility offered by God.

With each new step in life, I must try to discern where God is leading me. With my talents and abilities, my weaknesses and limitations, in my specific situation, what is God calling me to become? What new possibilities are open for me in this challenging moment? The Christian life becomes less an over-the-shoulder glance at the past and more a straining on tiptoes to chart the future. This is not to say that the past is unimportant. True creative change always brings into the present the richness of past tradition. However, the person who models himself or herself after a God who is the source of possibility is ready for the new.

Simply put, this book of poems and stories is all about faith. I do not understand faith as a set of doctrinal formulations or as adherence to a body of laws. For me, faith is a way of seeing. It is a mode of perception. The heart of faith is to see that God is at home here among us. In a sense, I have not written these poems and stories. They have written me. They have made me face the challenge of recognizing God in the eyes of a neighbor. They have called me to see God's hunger for justice in the hungry of our world. They have beckoned me to feel God's presence as I hold hands with my wife and hug my children.

It is not my vision that I share in these humble pages. It is a vision given to me by countless numbers of caring persons who have shared their perceptive insights in words and actions. I would like to thank especially my extended family and my community of fellow workers and students at Marian College who have supported and challenged my faith. So many have passed on to me their way of seeing, their challenge, their recognition of God. I pass on this vision because it is only together that we can see rightly.

WINTER

WINTER

Winter is a season of paradox. It boasts of shivering cold and friendly warmth. On the outside, this season is icy and stone-faced. But on the inside, there is security and strength in huddling close by a fire or wrapping ourselves in blankets as we sit and stare at twinkling lights on a Christmas tree. When we reflect on our paradoxical feelings about this season, we find that both the cold and the warmth are appreciated, for both call forth the child in us. There is nothing more exhilarating and wondrous than a blizzard when the season shuts down all the clatter of our commerce. There is nothing more awe-full than the glistening, frost-flocked trees after an ice storm. The snow and ice call us out into gleeful play, to forget the thermometer reading and to remember the days when mittened hands never got cold until they ached for hot chocolate.

Winter has a way of gathering us. It encourages us to experience the closeness of home, to find the warmth that comes only from each other. The child in us craves the cuddling, snuggling times that winter calls us to celebrate.

But winter is more than cold and warmth. It is also a season of waiting. It challenges us to recognize that we live in the not-yet kingdom that is never complete so long as we breathe. It is not a passive waiting, but a straining, expectant search for new life and deeper meaning. In the midst of winter comes the ever-new answer to our searching — Christmas. That which we dare not dream is fulfilled in the fragile flesh of a child who is God among us. Yet, even at Christmas, we are struck by the cold and the warmth of this season. The Christmas stable reminds us of all the doors we've slammed on the hopes and needs of the powerless poor. The Messiah's manger bed calls to mind the homeless and the oppressed who are still turned away. But the warmth of Christmas conquers the cold. The power of this defenseless child instills hope and confidence in the faithful love of God. With mouths wide open we gaze again at this tender trinity in Bethlehem, and we know that we cannot even guess the surprises that are yet to come.

PROMISE OF LOVE

To have dared to dream
the unimaginable moment
of God's son become man
was merely unminded fantasy.

To have the dream promised
from century to century
with prophetic poundings
on the door
of our unhoped hopes
marked history with desert cries.

To have the promise
child-like fulfilled
in stable, straw,
warm and whispered flesh
fixes us on tiptoes,
straining eyes to sight
the undared dawn.

All our fantasies
falter at this
largest lump of
jocund joy
caught in the throat
of time.

The lion and lamb
lie friendly now
and we
can love.

Isaiah 11:1-9

JOY ENOUGH

Smelling of donkey,
eyes caked with dust,
the young man pleads
for lodging and bread.

The woman waits —
hands fisted in fear.
"Why Bethlehem? Why now?"
she whispers to the sinking sun.

Joseph's empty eyes
betray the story of
slammed doors and curses.

He brings a
single, dry crust
and the promise
of a stable.

In the drafty stall
the feathered edges
of candlelight and night
shift with the wind
until newborn lungs
wail against the dark world.

They cuddle the
fragile flesh
in blankets
warmed by cattle's breath.

The dry crust
broken in midnight moments
speaks joy enough —
no less than love,
no more than hope.

Luke 2:1-7

CHRISTMAS STORY

The too-familiar story
twists and turns
in its retellings
as if no single scene
could capture truth.

Matthew's wise men
gaze at a dancing star.
Luke's shepherds
talk of angel skies.
And John speaks only of a word.

Christmas is easier
through children's eyes;
they do not argue with the tale.
Lions and lambs play peacefully
in the fairy-tale corners
of their minds.
Kisses cure in seconds
the hurts that will not heal in us.

We are stuck with swords
and plowshares;
friendly fences that scar
the landscape of hearts;
and walls that stand like
sentinels guarding our suspicion.

Only eyes as clear as laughter
can catch the common thread
woven in Christmas stories
old and new —
the soft and fragile flesh,
defenseless as a child.

Isaiah 9:5-6

18

GOD WAITS

We surround
the simple stable
with a glow of godly light.

We fill the sky
with winged angels
and a supernatural star.

Shepherds come with questions
about a heavenly king,
and magi march
a thousand desert miles,
bringing golden gifts.

But I think
the bundled bag lady
warming her weary feet
on the sewer grate
knows best
the naked truth
about that night —

the clammy warmth
of cattle's breath,

the beggar's share
of borrowed straw,

the fragile frailty
of life.

The tinsel in our story
hides the hard message
of stable-birth —

that God waits,
weeping and powerless
as a newborn babe,
for a word of welcome.

Luke 2:8-20

Matthew 1:18-2

JOSEPH

From last year's crumpled words,
we unwrap the young mother,
the newborn joy, the silent Joseph —
hoping that these months surrounded
by newspaper haven't soiled their story.

We know the mother well —
the young cheeks blushing
at the suggestion of the angel,
the yes-full heart that
makes Christmas was and now.

We know the babe,
whom shepherds, kings and
every child with a heart
will crowd to see.

And, then, there is this silent one.
He stands strongly by.
His brow is furrowed
with the questions and the dreams
that bring him to this stable.

His calloused hands
reveal his daily care of carpentry.
He knows the strength and weakness
of the wood —
a gift well-wished upon his son.

There is the faintest smile
settled like a snowflake on his lips
but he takes no attention to himself —
so we are asked to be.

THE SIMPLE STORY

A pregnant young girl,
pulled on a donkey
through the gray cold
by a tattered and tender
carpenter who can't
even find a room . . .

Here are all the signs
of insignificance.

A simple, crying child
stable-born,
warmed by straw
and cattle's breath . . .

He would die a
common criminal
hung on a cross.

But history would
never forget,
and those who believe in him
can still hear newborn cries
in the humble places
of their hearts.

Philippians 2:6-11

PROMISES AND STARS

With the certainty of trembling,
a few cold-cramped shepherds
believed that all the seeds
of centuries of hope
could blossom
with the birth
of a simple babe,
stable-born.

And three foolish men
crossed the continent
with camels full of gifts
because they trusted
in a surprising star.

I pray to be
a bit more shepherd-wise
and king-crazy,
to have sight enough
for dancing stars
and hope enough
for promises.

Matthew 2:1-12; Luke 2:11-20

23

BORN TO LIVE

We touch him — a minute old.

He breathes in whispers
as his large eyes
reach into our fragile hopes
and quiet prayers.

No bright star shatters the night.
No angel-song rings
on a shepherd hillside.
But wrinkled fingers,
strong as trust,
grasp our open hands.

Born into the darkness
of weapons and fear,
we wrap him in warm promises
and set our hearts
on the dawn of peace.

John 1:1-11

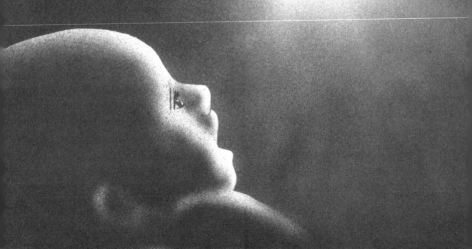

NEW YEAR

Just a moment before midnight,
before we sip the kindness cup
of memories and promises,
before the first snowflake
clings crystal-sure to
the eyelid of another year,
for one breath-long moment
we drink deep of that moist silence
when lips meet —
and a new world begins
with wordless wonder.

Song of Songs 1:1-4 or 1 John 1:1-5

REMEMBER

This was not the first time that Victor Paschal had climbed Mount Temple, but it might be the last — if he made it to the summit. Two previous times he had attempted the climb. The first time it was a biting, blinding storm that had forced the team to give up. The second time, his friend and teacher had died when an avalanche of snow and ice struck him full force in the chest, causing internal injuries so severe that he had not survived the rescue attempt.

As Vic and his team set up base camp, he recalled his friend's patience during the endless hours of practice he had spent with Vic. It was not just climbing Vic had learned, but the meaning of a challenge and the joy of friendship.

On Friday, the weather was clear and cold — no forecast of heavy snows. Vic and four other climbers began their ascent. With each carefully placed step, Vic remembered the life of giving that his friend had shared with him. His thoughts carried him back to the day when he had dangled between life and death, held by the lifeline of his friend. A gaping crevice had opened underneath his feet and only the courage and expert judgment of his friend had saved him.

Friday went without a hitch, although the day was long and exhausting. From here on, each member of the team would wear a transceiver, a small radio device that sends or receives a radio signal. Team members could locate anyone caught in an avalanche by listening to his radio tone. As they climbed, the team would listen carefully for the hollow thud of snow that might warn of an avalanche.

On Saturday, a light sifting snow began to fall — not enough to hamper the climbers. It reminded Vic of a similar snow several years earlier when he had climbed his first real mountain. He could almost hear again the words of his friend who had stood beside him, "You will conquer even greater peaks than this. You were meant for this feeling of triumph close to the clouds."

Saturday's journey led the team to the base of a sheer, cold wall — the final, tormenting challenge of this mountain. Before falling asleep, Victor reflected on the summit — what would he leave behind as a remembrance of his teacher and friend?

Sunday's challenge took all the strength each person had.

Every step up the icy rock was followed by exhaustion. The team measured its progress in inches. Three hours of picking out footholds and securing lifelines brought them to the peak. As Victor set foot on the top of this part of the world, he half-whispered, half-panted a prayer for his friend. Each man jammed into the snow on the summit a small red flag bearing his victorious name. On Vic's flag, there were two names. He had not climbed this mountain alone.

Acts 3:1-16

WITH EYES WIDE OPEN

Jon Optler couldn't have been happier. He had sunk the winning shot from the top of the key against his school's greatest rival just eight hours before. After spending the night at a friend's house, he was headed home to go ice fishing with his dad. His dad wanted to get started early, so it was an hour before sunrise on a crisp morning in January when Jon decided to take the back road into town. He was thinking about the split second before the buzzer when his eyes had focused on the hoop and his arms had pumped the ball with just the right arch. He saw the "Caution — 35 m.p.h." sign too late. He was going at least 50 when he started into the sharp curve on County Trunk N. He felt the car slide across the pavement, spin and nose dive into the gulley on the side of the road. His head slammed into the steering wheel, and Jon immediately lost consciousness.

When Jon awoke twenty minutes later, all was blackness and pain. He blinked his eyes again and again, but he couldn't see. His left leg, throbbing with pain, was pinned between the steering wheel and the cold metal of the car. He felt helpless and afraid. He heard a large truck coming down the road. He felt a surge of hope when the truck downshifted and braked to a stop just above him. He listened to the opening of the truck door, a frantic tearing through the branches, and then, a strong deep voice next to his left ear. "It's okay, kid. Just hang in there; we'll get you out of this mess. I've already called for help. My name is Billy. How are you feelin'?"

"I can't see, man, and I'm cold. My left leg is pinned in here, and I can't see."

"I'll get you a blanket."

"No, don't leave me!"

"It's okay, I'll just be gone a minute; I'll be right back."

Jon could hear the man running up the bank. The truck door opened. The man talked on his radio, but Jon couldn't make out the words. And then, Jon heard Billy running toward him again. Billy carefully wrapped a heavy blanket around Jon. He rested his arm on Jon's shoulder and pressed what felt like a feather into Jon's hand, which was still tightly gripping the steering wheel.

"You hold on to this eagle feather, Son. It's a sign of the Great Spirit. My grandfather gave it to me when I was about your age. He was an Apache medicine man, and he always told me that the Great Spirit gives us the courage to get through anything."

Jon was glad not to be alone. Somehow, the pain and fear weren't quite as bad with someone there.

"Thanks, Billy," was all Jon could mutter through his clenched teeth as the waves of pain flowed through him. Jon relaxed his hand a little on the steering wheel. He felt the soft edges of the feather and prayed that the blackness in front of his eyes would go away. It seemed like an eternity before the sharp scream of sirens stopped Billy's gentle talking. It took ten minutes to pry Jon out of the wreckage. All the while, he clasped the eagle feather in his right fist and hoped that he would see again.

As the attendants slid the stretcher into the ambulance, Billy was there at the door to say good-bye. "You just hang on to that feather, Son. I'll come collect it tomorrow. Good luck."

A team of doctors met Jon at the hospital. Jon's breathing was regular. There didn't seem to be any internal bleeding and only a few external scrapes and minor cuts, but his body temperature was dangerously low. As they wrapped him in heated blankets, one of the doctors remarked, "You were very lucky that truck driver showed up; you couldn't have taken that cold too much longer."

Later, another doctor, an ophthalmologist, explained to Jon that there were no foreign objects in his eyes. "I think when your head slammed into the steering wheel, the area of the brain where sight is registered was severely bruised. But we'll do some more checking later when you're stabilized."

Next, Jon heard his dad calling his name. His mother grasped Jon's hand and felt the feather which he gripped tightly in his sweating palm. Jon explained about Billy, the eagle feather and the Great Spirit. "I can't see, Mom. Will I ever play basketball again? Billy said the Great Spirit .... " But Jon couldn't say anymore. The pain was too much; he tightened his jaw against the stabbing blackness. And then, he realized that basketball wasn't really so important. He would never again take for granted these two loving people beside him. Also, if he could see again, he'd take the time to thank God every day for the sunrise.

Later in the day, X-rays revealed that Jon's left leg was broken. A doctor set the leg and applied a cast. A brain scan revealed that a small blood vessel had broken in his brain. A pocket of blood had formed, putting pressure on one area of Jon's brain and preventing him from seeing. The pressure would have to be relieved. The neurosurgeon scheduled an operation for the next morning.

Jon's parents prayed with him before the operation.

"Dad, they won't let me take this feather into the operating room; would you hold on to it for me? Remember, the Great Spirit will get us through this."

When Jon came out of the anesthetic five hours later, his mumbled words brought tears of joy. "I can see, I can see!" And what he saw were three jubilant faces. In between Jon's mom and dad stood Billy, clutching the eagle feather in his large hands.

A special note of thanks goes to Doctor Fred Karsten for his generous help in the preparation of this story.

John 9:1-41

SPRING

SPRING

S pring is a season of passion. There is an urge, an energy in spring that cannot be contained. Bright blossoms spring up between rocks, break out of hard, cold soil and lavish their grace on unsuspecting passersby. Robins ruffle their feathers against the uncertain chill and dare to proclaim the arrival of new life. Young men take off their shirts on their way home from school on days that would be called cold in August. Everywhere there is greenness. Porches are full of people released from the imprisoned darkness of winter. The days lengthen, and once again the racket of children playing outdoors echoes into evening.

In all of this passionate activity, the Easter message heralds itself loud and clear — death shall have no dominion. Life is a promise made by a God who keeps promises. Light is victorious and nothing can conquer it. Joy is the final outcome, and no amount of sadness will dim its exultation. Our journeys through sorrow and pain do not end in despair. Our experiences of loss and hurt are not the final chapter. The drama of life is a comedy, not a tragedy. The final sound is not a whimper, but the full-throated laugh of one who knows a God who transforms cocoons into butterflies and sinfulness into the opportunity for salvation.

SPRING FEVER

All in a rush
comes spring —
robins multiply like
beginning brush strokes
on a gray-green canvas of lawn.

Crocuses emerge
chick-like from a brown
shell of cold earth.

Rivulets,
freed from icy slavery,
run in veins
and explode into a million
capillaries of wetness.

And a familiar
longing fever
rises in my blood.

Psalm 147

DEATH OF A FARMER
(For Uncle Bill)

His dreams were close to reality,
his hands accustomed to callouses,
his sufferings were only a little
out of the ordinary.

A man of simple speech
whose vision was tempered
by climate,
projected rainfall,
and expected sunshine.

No great names telegraph
or arrange the quickest flight.
Only those close to the soil,
clad in Sunday shoes,
talk of seeding and pasture.

They gather on the day of ashes
to lower a friend to dust,
knowing that he has been tested
by the weather of many seasons.

They are well-acquainted with harvest —
the season of timeless truth.

1 Thessalonians 4:13-18

BIRCHES

Silver,
then white again.
As a spring moon
shimmers,
mammoth tusks stand
silhouetted
against the black and burnt
desolation
of forest.
I walk amid
the ivory tusks
on a battlefield
where the fallen lay
and wonder
how this courageous bark
dares to stand
so straight
and tall
and white.

Colossians 3:12-15

A LAYER OF ICE THICKER

Two years ago
calendars didn't need
to crow-call the spring.

The season's first green days
seeped through
discarded, blackened snow
to bone-deep truth.

A touch of orange
upon the robin's breast
could bud the barren branch.

A few drops
of warm rain could
houseclean a city.

But every year,
a layer of ice thicker,
we ask for more proof.

Colossians 2:6-15

LAST SIGNS OF WINTER

The last traces of snow,
like old crumpled newspapers
strewn in corners by a rough wind.

A flock of blown leaves,
surviving the winter
chatters against the pavement.

Ice thins and finally gives up
against the rush of
warm spring fever.

Tulips peak through
in sunny shelters
and dare to
proclaim the promise
of new seasons.

Revelation 21:1-4

THE WATCHING WINDOW

On a labor-built nest,
courageous patience
warms the three blue promises
of new life.
Unafraid of a thousand stares
and curious glances,
she knows it is only
this persistent tenderness
which brings openness
and gives freedom
to fragile wings
hoping to fly.

Philippians 1:3-11

FOR EMILY
ON BAPTISMAL DAY

Emily,
we pray in water signs
of simple hope
the touch of God
upon your life —
a greening touch
of goodness, grace,
and constant growth.

We'd love to give you
a world of
pure white peace
and fearless freedom,
but all we have
are promises.

We cradle you
in human hands,
sadly sure
of our imperfections.

But, we vow forever
to keep on trying —
to make the world
a peaceful place
and earth
more like the kingdom.

Ephesians 6:10-17

ONE TIMELESS MAN

One timeless man,
twisted upon the cross
of time, crucified
in the nightmare
of a moment,
trusted
and split the
centuries in two:
before his coming,
after his death.
Tired and tortured,
he hung
for an eternity
upon a black cross
in the cold
wooden sky,
thirsting for a time
when
meaning would rise
with every sun,
when salvation
would swallow suffering.
Time laughed for an hour
while men played games;
the second hour
they whispered;
the third,
waited.
The clouds gathered
like a flock of
silent birds,
the sun turned
blood;
time stopped,
stunned by a cry
of confusion and confidence,
halted by a trumpet blast
of trust.
Silence shouted
into darkness,
and time began again
with a moment of meaning,
a new-day dawn of promise,
and the rising sun
enlightened
trusting man.

Colossians 1:15-20

THE VOICE OF GOD

Once, there was a young man who wished to hear the voice of God. He imagined that God's voice must be great and mighty. Carrying only a few small loaves of bread, he set off on his journey to hear the voice of God.

First, he traveled to the ocean. He stood on the shore, where the powerful waves pounded constantly against the rugged bare rocks. The sound of the mammoth waves smashing against the granite was deafening! He had never heard such a thunderous sound. In the deafening noise, he lost himself, but he did not hear the voice of God. The young man thought, therefore, that God's voice must be greater still.

He journeyed to a huge waterfall on the edge of nowhere. The wall of churning water fell for a thousand feet. It crashed to the earth with such unimaginable force that it shook the ground and the sky. The roar of the waterfall drained the strength from the young man. Surely, he thought, this must be the voice of God. As he listened, however, he heard only his own heart throbbing inside him.

Finally, he traveled to the highest mountain peak he could find. There he waited for God to speak in peals of thunder. On the third day after his arrival, gray, heavy clouds darkened the sky. The clouds hung so low above the earth that they seemed to surround him. About noon, the sky was split in two by a lightening bolt, and the silence was shattered by a roar of thunder. The young man could not bear the sound, which was like a drum beating and cymbal clashing and a trumpet blowing, all at once, inside his skull. This must be the voice of God, the young man thought. But as he listened, he only became more afraid, and he was certain that this could not be the voice of God. Holding his head, which throbbed with pain, the young man lost no time climbing down the mountain.

He was exhausted and disappointed that his journey had come to nothing. He had searched everywhere he knew, and still he had not heard the voice of God. He retreated into the forest at the bottom of the mountain and found a dry spot under a huge oak where he could rest. As he clutched his last small loaf of bread, sleep came quickly.

While the young man slept, he dreamed of a simple woman who could quiet the ocean with a gentle prayer. He dreamed that this woman was able to stop the waterfall with a wave of her hand and silence the thunder with a single word.

The young man was startled awake by the twitter of birds.

As he opened his eyes, he noticed the fresh sunlight filtering through the branches of the oak. Then he heard the sound of footsteps coming in his direction. The young man felt as if his dream were becoming real. He looked in the direction of the footsteps. There, however, he saw only a weary old man with unshaven face and drooping eyelids. As the stranger plodded closer, the young man could see hunger and pain written on the man's face. The stranger took a few more steps and then fell in a crumpled heap at the feet of the young man. From deep within the old man came a single word, "Bread." As the young man broke his last small loaf to feed the stranger, he knew that he had heard the voice of God.

Luke 24:13-35

NEVER END

Kimberly had been awake most of the night, going through the jumps and turns in her mind, tracing the figures with the tip of her toe on the bed sheets. Tomorrow, the final stage of the Olympic figure skating tryouts would find her more than ready.

It seemed as if her whole life had been a preparation for this day. She recalled the story of her third Christmas. Her mom and dad had told the story to her at least a hundred times — how she had frantically ripped the red-striped paper off the heavy box and had found her first pair of figure skates. Kimberly didn't actually remember that Christmas day so many years ago — but she had relived her childish delight through the words of her parents.

She did remember enrolling for figure-skating lessons when she was almost five. During those first years of lessons, skating was sheer fun. It was something new, and she seemed to be a "natural" at the sport. However, there were times in later years when the lessons and the practices became drudgery. Her classmates were getting involved in band, chorus and scouting. The only thing that kept Kimberly's interest was the excitement of the area figure skating competitions.

Kimberly remembered the first time she saw television coverage of the Winter Olympics. Day after day she watched the figure skating competition and the graceful moves of the gold medalist. It was then that she decided, "That's what I want to do." She entered into her lessons with more energy and purpose than ever. She looked forward to state and regional competitions with an eye to the Olympics.

The practice was sometimes grueling, and at times she doubted her own ability. She reflected on her first attempt at a triple-toe loop when she went sprawling on the ice. For weeks after that, it seemed that half her body was black and blue. Still she kept trying to master more difficult moves. Only the insistence and encouragement of her instructor made her continue.

Her practices, the thousands of hours spent going over and over her routines, her bumps and bruises, the risk of trying new combinations — all this had brought her to this day. This was her goal, her dream. This was the end of all her preparations.

The jangle of her alarm clock startled Kimberly out of her daydreaming. As she sat up and rubbed her eyes, she thought to herself, "If I make this Olympic team, it won't be the end; it will just be a new beginning."

Proverbs 4:18-27

SUMMER

SUMMER

Summer is the season of sunshine and festivity. It is a time for re-creation. We step out of our usual routine to explore the lush greenery of life that we so often pass by. We slow our hectic pace to appreciate the gifts of creation that surround us.

So much of our culture is focused on domination and control. We get caught up in plans and projects. We become enamored with our own technology. But summer calls us to recognize that all we have is gift — that our deepest insights and most clever plans are not our creations alone. Summer challenges us to realize that we are made to live in harmony with the universe rather than to dominate it. Our survival and that of our planet may well depend on our learning this lesson of respect.

Such respect has its source in wonder. It is the experience of wonder that opens our eyes to the fragile balance of our world and the tender care of our God. Wonder has us recognize the inextricable connection among all things. As we watch the careful spinning of the spider or the persistent patience of the mother robin or the reckless explorations of a child, we come to know the profound unity of the universe and the one God, whose love shines through every miraculous, ordinary event.

SUMMER THREE

Summer is chocolate ice cream,
melted by 33 flavors of sun
and running down the side
of a crisp cone,
down to the elbow
and dripping on a tanned tummy,
three years old.

And black seeds,
tongue-twisted out of
a smile of red watermelon
and spit twenty feet
("But I can eat the white seeds, Dad.")
and the proud shout,
"My feet can touch the pedals."

Matthew 19:13-15

LISTEN TO THE WARM
(To Rod McKuen)

A silent tree stands
meditating a moonlight.
Between its gnarled fingers
it holds the golden orb
whose fragile syllables
of whispered light
find me still awake,
gently impatient
to listen to the warm,
knowing that not so far away
one is sleeping
who shares the warmth
of me.

Song of Songs 1:15-2:7 or 1 John 4:16-18

50

REFLECTIONS AROUND A CAMPFIRE

Today, you and I
walked the trails
of mind and meadow,
maneuvered through the deep
underbrush of
wild woods and wonderings.

With all the imagining
of a bareback August sun,
we pretended to be hunters
when we spied
the innocent deer tracks.
Stepping softly,
we hoped to steal
an arrow's glance at truth.

But, tonight,
with sore legs
resting on the warm stones
that ring our campfire,
there is no time for pretending.

We've pitched our tent
in each other's land
and we are home —
wherever that may lead us.

Genesis 2:18-25

BIRTHDAY

No matter the number of years.
Life leads always
to the moment of now,
where past and future
gather in the almost
motionless motion of the pendulum.

Here is the beginning
and the end—
the reason for both.

The moment is quicker
than lightning
before the wash of warm rain
reaches the sun-streaked window.

Vision begins in the I of now,
the kiss drawn deep
from the heart of promise
and prayer too subtle for sound.

Birth is always a journey
just begun.

Psalm 20:1-6

LANGUAGE OF LOVE

It is a language
never spoken,
too powerful and frail
for speech,
too intricate for syntax,
but your hands and eyes
keep calling me.

Song of Songs 4:9-16 or 1 John 4:7-11

THE WEB OF FRIENDSHIP

The web of friendship,
spider-like,
is woven with silent
and mostly invisible
strands,
small thread-like
hands
that are forever
reaching
to find the gentle
grasp
that signs a bridge
between two hearts,
stronger
than sacred steel structures
(products of mathematical
and calculating minds),
a bridge
that spans the space
of souls,
that links
in freedom
hearts
straining with visions,
questions, goals.

This little creature
knows not why
it builds the web
or why it builds here.
It only knows
to build
and therefore
be.

1 John 4:19-21

UNTITLED

Like the in-between time,
when night rises into morning
and the first bird
tries its untuned voice,
and I am unsure
if dreams are real,

Certainty
is such a
delicate gift,
given only by the
thorn
of time.

Ecclesiastes 3:1-8

A SMILE

No mask
of painted hypocrisy

or facade
of loud laughter
rather she
blessed me
with resurrection
upon her lips

that sign
of new-life joy
perhaps
the secret
shared
by friends
that you

are more
than only you

being also
part of me. . . .

1 Corinthians 12:12-26

EUCHARIST

We are the wheat
gathered from the hillsides,
gathered from the valleys,
gathered into one.

We are the wheat
gathered and chosen,
crushed and sifted,
molded into one.

We are the dough
kneaded and risen,
molded and shaped,
baked into one.

We are the bread
blessed and broken,
shared and eaten,
offered as one.

We are the Eucharist,
one as Christ's body,
given for each other,
the bread of love.

1 Corinthians 11:23-26

REMEMBER

John was seventeen, the oldest son of Mr. and Mrs. Peter Jason. His mom and dad were pretty good parents, he thought. They were a bit too strict sometimes, but John knew that they really did care about him and his brothers and sisters. Lately, John had been thinking a great deal about his relationship with his parents because his father had cancer. The cancer was discovered two years ago when John's dad went to the doctor for a routine checkup. The doctor found a large growth under Mr. Jason's left arm and told him that it might be cancerous. The usual tests were performed. The tumor was found to be malignant; it had to be removed.

John did not understand much about the operation at the time because his parents were very quiet about the whole thing. The doctor told Mr. Jason that the cancer seemed to be arrested, but that it might spread to other parts of his body.

After the operation, Mr. Jason called their first family reunion. From three states, aunts and uncles and cousins and grandparents came for the reunion. The Jason family had not had such a gathering for a very long time. Mr. Jason made plans to have the family gather together every year for a summer celebration.

John was not particularly enthusiastic about the idea of spending a whole weekend with relatives, some of whom he didn't even know. He did enjoy the campfires, though, and the many stories that Grandpa Jason told to the whole group after the little children were put to bed. These stories made John feel as if he were part of a history, part of a life bigger than his own. His dad told John that these family reunions made him feel the same way. It was a way of remembering.

Both John and his dad enjoyed the special foods the aunts and uncles spent hours preparing. Uncle George always made a five-gallon pail of minty iced tea. And every year he would talk about how his mother had taught him to pick the freshest stalks of mint and to buy the freshest lemons to get the right flavor. Grandma Jason had been dead for several years, but she seemed to be with them all at family reunion time when Uncle George served his iced tea.

Two weeks before the family's third reunion, John's dad went in for his periodic checkup. This time, the doctor's diagnosis was not good news. The cancer in Mr. Jason's body was spreading through his glands. John's dad didn't know whether another operation would be required. He didn't know if he could expect to live very long. He looked forward more than ever to the family's third reunion, when he could reminisce about all that his life had meant.

John looked forward to the family reunion, too. For some reason, he wanted to hear the stories again. But more, he wanted to know that his father would be remembered in a special way in the family reunions to come.

John 13:1-15

THREE PLUS ONE EQUALS

Steve Peterson was ten and an only child. Perhaps there are advantages to being an only child — your own room, no little brothers or sisters to follow you around, maybe even a little more spending money. But Steve was looking forward to having a brother or sister. Ever since his parents had filed for adoption two years earlier, he had wondered what it would be like to share his world with another member of the family.

Then the Petersons received a call from the adoption agency. A five-year-old boy needed a home. Immediately after getting the call, Pam Peterson called her husband at work. There were many things to get ready to welcome a new child into the family. That night Steve and his parents went shopping for clothes and bedroom furniture. Steve insisted that they buy a baseball uniform that was on sale. He thought that his brother should have one.

The Petersons were up extra early on the adoption day. It was a day they would remember with joy and would celebrate with parties for many years. Steve's dad would remember the firm handshake he received from his new son, David. And they would repeat over and over David's ecstatic comment when he walked into his new bedroom, "Oh, great — bunkbeds!"

After dinner that night, Steve played catch with David. When Steve's mom called out the window that his best friend was on the phone and wanted him to come over for a while, Steve said, "Tell him I'll see him tomorrow." Steve knew that he had much to learn about love for and responsibility to this new member of the family.

It would be a few months before David felt really comfortable in his new home. It would take time to learn about the ways in which these people loved and accepted him. Along with that love and acceptance would come the expectations and responsibilities of being a son — school work, chores, the kisses Mom loved at his bedtime and many other things. But this first night, there was just one question David had to ask. After he settled into the bottom bunk and Mom and Dad tucked him in and the lights were turned off, David dared his question.

"Are you going to be my big brother now?"

"Yes," came the reply from the bed above, "forever."

1 John 2:3-10

AUTUMN

AUTUMN

Saying good-bye is never easy. Letting go always involves pain. There is no other way with life. To deny suffering and loss would be to turn our backs on growth and challenge. Change is most often experienced as a threat to our security and the status quo. Autumn is the season of prophets when we hear the upsetting challenge to change, to die. It is a season that disturbs our comfortableness. We all know the necessity of death, but we often shrink from the necessity of our own dyings.

We can learn an important lesson from the vibrant color of this autumn season. Death is not without its joy and celebration. The season takes delight in letting go. There is a certain playfulness in the dancing leaves as they fall to earth in their annual journey to ashes. Autumn knows that from these ashes new beginnings will arise, new friendships will blossom, new meanings will take root in us. Autumn calls us to trust the rhythm of creation and the wisdom of the Creator.

(like dreams)

a
fall(en)
leaf
withered brown
by
age
and now
two seasons
old
still clings
to an
old
pair of shoes
like dreams
(like dreams)
that do (not?)
die
but s-l-o-w-l-y
drop
from the soul
piece
by
piece. . . .

Ecclesiastes 1:4-11

REVELATION

I've been out
crushing acorns,
stepping cruelly
on the hard,
brown-capped seed
until the shell
cracks open and
reveals
a pure white
secret.

Wisdom 7:1-14

A SIMPLE QUESTION

Into now
rush all the risks and worries
of promises and prayers,
all the frail beginnings
in times even unremembered.
The well-plotted plans
that reach with fragile fingers
toward the unopened
and the distant music
that played round and round
the painted carousel
all gather now
to sit beside me
in night's close corner,
to pose a simple question.

My world waits
for one man's meaning,
a softly-spoken word,
your name.

Song of Songs 3:1-4 or 1 John 2:24-25

AUTUMN MEMORIES

A fleet of yellow raincoats
bob up and down
on a river of rain,
rushing down to the windy corner.

There the children huddle close
until the splashing cars pass,
and then, string out in playfulness again.

The gray sky hugs me,
and the smell of
the first fires of fall
is on her breath.

And the taste of hot chocolate
sipped from a thermos
clings like an autumn leaf
to the wet windowpane
of my memory.

Mark 10:13-16

THE TOIL OF LOVE

In every turn of my mind
I find
in the furrows of its fertile soil
the toil
that placed these persistent seeds.

Not in a moment of readiness
to bless
this stubborn, hardened clay,
but day
by day you softened me.

Clump by clump you held and broke
and spoke
the life within this dirt
and hurt,
which was the only way.

Mark 4:1-9

GOOD-BYE, FATHER

And now I must walk again upon
this land of fallen
colored leaves.

You, my father,
colored with the years
and seasons,
lie fallen from
the tree of life....
slowly to be trodden into
earth,
the soil of my growth,
as this tree of me
reaches out for sunlight,
stretches to a larger shadow
to please the passersby.

1 Thessalonians 4:14-18

I AM NOT WORTHY

Must there be
in everyone
a knot
in the smooth,
well-grained,
obedient wood,
a knot
which no amount
of sanding or chiseling
can erase?

No, you cannot see
the damned spot.
I've covered it
with harsh,
splintering bark
so you are afraid
to approach it.

All the tree of me
has been stripped bare
to show the smoothness
and the life except
for one damned spot.

Will the sculptor
chisel around it,
or will he
just discard the wood?
Can the artist use
an imperfect piece?

Perhaps,
the thing
he shapes of me
must need
a knot.

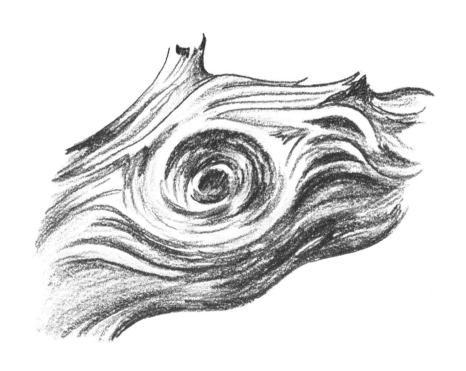

Psalm 139

AUTUMN SECRET

I was startled awake by the close honking of geese. This was nature's kind intrusion of a lazy afternoon's dream. The double-syllable call told me they were Canadas. As I ran outside to see the winged migration, I felt, for the first time, the coldness of the late-October breezes. The true prophets of the approaching winter shouted their warnings of ice and snow. They were winging high and strongly, the skirmish line led by an old gander, wise in the ways and dangers of travel and rigidly insistent on obedience to his honked orders.

Suddenly the V-formation arrowed toward the dazzling surface of the pond.

The large Canada honkers braced themselves for the landing. They kept balance with outstretched necks, braking their flight with fanned tails and flailing their wings to cut their speed. The big birds played touch-and-go with the sparkling surface. Their feet and tails furrowed the water as they set their enormous wings in a gliding position to stabilize their bodies. Then, they raised their heads to their normal poses and settled their weight amid the spray, safe.

I ran to see what autumn secret these eloquent messengers could bring. The graceful sky gliders floated silently, listening and alert. Their giant webbed feet made them smooth and graceful swimmers. With long necks straining, they continued their cautious observation. They did not trust this little man-made pond. A pulse of nervousness seemed to ripple through the little group as they ruffled their brown plumage. Their heavy bodies were boldly patterned, with a broad white band across throat and cheeks. Occasionally, one would dip under water to nibble the roots of an aquatic plant. They seemed to splash a child-like game, but it was not fun for them. For some reason, they could not find the peace they wanted.

It looked as though they sniffed the air with the sagacity and wariness of a good hound.

Their caution was interrupted, however, as a bitter blast of gunshot echoed in the woods. They did not hesitate to ask the meaning of this noise, but off they were with frenzied flapping of wings. There was plenty of talking in the ranks as they took off, some with a quick run, others with only a leap into the air.

They pounded their powerful wings against the stiffness of the breeze. They climbed and climbed, perhaps desiring to hide within the whiteness of the clouds. Finally, the honking Canadas leveled off to find another, more perfect refuge for a rest. Before they silhouetted themselves in the crisp October sky, they left their autumn secret rippled in the water: "You were made to rule but also love."

Genesis 1:20-31

JOURNEY IN YOUR MIND

It is early afternoon on a rainy autumn day. The rain splashes gently in puddles, runs silently down the trunks of trees and makes them shine in the dull light of a cloudy day. It seems cold and damp for fall, but you decide to take a walk. Something seems to be calling you to explore the woods and paths that lie outside before you.

You put on a soft warm sweater, your favorite color, and it makes you feel snug against the damp chill of the afternoon. Then, you put on a raincoat, and you are ready for your journey.

You leave this room, and you are alone. You are happy to have the time just to walk by yourself and think. As you walk across the grass, you notice how a few angleworms have slithered out of the soft soil. You notice rain running down the hill. You wonder where these little streams of water will end — perhaps in the ocean, many, many days from here. Perhaps the little streams will evaporate into the air and will rain down upon some other part of this wide world.

You walk into the woods. It seems warmer in the woods for some reason. You follow a well-worn path. The colorful leaves of the trees seem to shelter you. The ground seems to cushion your feet; in some spots you can hear the squishing of the wet dirt beneath your step. You notice the different colors of the tree trunks — the dark, dark brown, the smooth gray of the aspen, the white and black of the birch.

To the right of you is a large birch that seems to have been here forever. There are two words carved into the wood. The words are hard to make out, but, after looking awhile, you read them and you wonder who has been here before you. Someone has left a message carved in the trunk of this tree, and you have received it. You store the message in your mind and continue along the path, which seems to be getting narrower.

You notice now, that there are more and more pines growing in this part of the woods. The needles shine with wetness — a deep, dark green. You reach out to touch them, and they prick your hand. You take one of the long spear-like needles, and you bend it in two. When you break it, you notice the fresh scent of pine. The fragrance fills your nostrils.

There is a carpet of brown needles covering the ground underneath the pines. You decide to rest here awhile. You crouch underneath one of the large branches, and you feel warm and safe. You notice three small white mushrooms growing close to the trunk of the pine. You see a little black beetle slowly making its way across the brown pine needles. The way seems so difficult. You feel thankful that you were born into this world a person — with arms and legs and a mind and a heart. You try to listen to your heart beating inside you. You have to be very still, very quiet to hear your heart, which is keeping you alive.

You go a little farther into the woods after your short rest, and, all of a sudden, the path ends. You feel adventuresome today, and you decide to venture farther into the woods. To your left, you hear the sound of water falling over rocks — it must be a stream. You decide to follow the sound. You go a few yards toward the water, and you notice that there is a clearing ahead. It smells as though wood is burning now, and you notice a few puffs of smoke rising above the trees. Who could be here, in this lonely, forgotten spot?

You scramble a few more yards, ducking underneath branches and stepping over fallen limbs until you reach a clearing beside a gentle stream. You notice in the clearing that there is a soft carpet of fresh new grass already growing. The stream runs swiftly as it falls over shining white and black, pink and gray rounded pebbles. You look across the stream and see a lean-to made from pine branches. The smoke is rising from the lean-to, but you cannot see the fire. You can see only the back of the small shelter.

You decide to cross the stream and see who could be here. As you step from the stone in the middle of the stream to the opposite bank, a man steps out from the side of the shelter. He seems kind and gentle. He says, "Come, I have been waiting for you." You sit on a smooth warm log on one side of the fire, and he sits on the other side. You spend several moments just looking at each other. You notice his eyes and his face.

The fire is crackling and warm. You feel the fire's warmth on your legs. The man has a small loaf of bread. He takes the loaf, breaks it in half and hands one half to you. The bread is good and warm and sweet. Eating the man's bread is like sharing life with him.

After you have finished eating, the man looks at you with eyes full of peace and asks you one question. You are not sure what to answer, and you hesitate, so he asks the question again. You answer this time, slowly but surely. Then, the man gives you a simple message. He asks you to remember the message — one simple sentence to store away in your heart and to live by. You thank him for the message, and you notice that the sky is getting darker. You must leave.

You travel quickly on your return journey. After crossing the clear stream, you find the path again. You make your way through the dense pines and down the path that becomes wider and more traveled. With each step, the message that you were given sinks deeper into your being. You consider again his question, the look on his face and the simple challenge that he gave you.

Mark 8:27-30

79